How to Hitchhike from Texas to California in 3 Days in 14 Easy Steps

A True Story

by Judy Sheer Watters

Lived out by Kyle A. Watters

Illustrated by Katie Paul

FRANKLIN
SCRIBES
PUBLISHERS

Copyright ©2017 by Franklin Scribes Publishing

Author Webpage
judywatters.com

Facebook: Judy Sheer Watters, Author

Publisher's Author Page
franklinscribes.com/judy-sheer-watters

Amazon: The Road Home: The Legacy that was, is and is to Come

No part of this publication may be reproduced, distributed, or transmitted in any form or by any means, including photocopying, recording, or other electronic or mechanical methods, or by any information storage and retrieval system without the prior written permission of the publisher, except in the case of very brief quotations embodied in critical reviews and certain other noncommercial uses permitted by copyright law.

ISBN Paperback: 978-1-941516-24-9
ISBN ebook: 978-1-941516-14-0

This book was published thanks to free support and training from: EbookPublishingSchool.com

Dedication

I dedicate this book to Kyle, our youngest child, who has always had to live life his way. And to all the moms out there who have a Kyle and have learned the patience, bravery and unconditional love needed while their child searches for his own way in life.
May you be blessed.

Write and let me know about your Kyle.
sheermemoirs@gmail.com

How to Hitchhike
from Texas to California
in 3 Days
in 14 Easy Steps

STEP 1:

Notify your family

- Use these exact words: "Mom, I'm going to California."

- To which she will say, "Great idea, son. How will you get there?" She will think this to be a logical question considering you have no money and have not worked anywhere for six months.

- You will say, "Thought I would hitchhike. In fact, I'm leaving tonight."

- Mom will try to play it cool. Since you are over 18, she will not say no to you, but rather offer options. She will say, "California sounds exciting. Change of scenery, new friends—might be good for you. However, you might consider working at McDonalds for a few months till you get enough money for a bus ticket."

- At this point, you must be strong. You must say, "No, I have decided—I have to go tonight."

STEP 2:

Make every preparation necessary for the trip, even if you just decided five minutes before to hitchhike 1,354.2 miles.

- Call your old friend in California and see if you can stay with him until you find a job. His "yes" answer will spur you into top speed.

- Find every loose penny that is laying around your bedroom, and count out your whopping $6.00.

- Pack a very heavy backpack to include your laptop, charger, and shaver. Also, pack a gym bag to the point that it bulges out at the seams. This way, drivers will take pity on you and be more apt to stop and give you a ride.

- Since you are headed to California, pack lots of shorts and t-shirts. One pair of shoes should be enough—the pair you are wearing.

- Don't forget your cell phone and charger, so you can keep in touch with Mom. She will want a report as to your progress every hour on the hour, all night long.

- Say goodbye to your parents and Grandma.

- Grandma will cry. She will slip all the money she has into your hand (all $15.00).

- Give Grandma an extra hug and tell her you'll be okay.

STEP 3:

Ask your mom to drive you to the expressway.

- Since you live in the country, it's only reasonable that she would take you the 20 miles to the closest expressway.

- However, she might say, "I'm your Mom. I am not going to drop you off on the expressway in the middle of the night. If you want to get there, you will have to find another way."

- Since it is only two miles to the closest main road, you might try this strategy.

- "Mom, just take me out to the highway then."

- To which she will say, "California is a long way. Two miles isn't that far."

- She may add, "I have an appointment at 9:00 a.m. Don't call me from Kerrville then to ask me to come get you."

- Dad will say, "See you in an hour."

- Don't forget your phone.

STEP 4:

Walk to the end of the driveway.

- Turn back toward the house for a final look.
- Inhale; exhale.
- You are really doing this.
- Get to the neighbor's house and realize that since you lost your driver's license a few months before, you will need your passport for ID.
- Inhale; exhale.
- Turn around and go back to the house.
- The door will be locked—already.
- Ring doorbell.
- Dad will say, "Back already?"
- Ignore his comment; find your passport and leave again.

STEP 5:

Wait until dark to leave home and wear jeans and a black hooded jacket.

- This is especially helpful if you are in the country and have to walk two miles to get to the main road. If a neighbor sees you, they will surmise that you are either selling drugs or robbing houses. Either way, they will summon the police to your rescue.

- When you see the blue flashing lights coming up over the hill, just one mile from home, grab your cell phone to call Mom.

- But don't panic; be cool. Don't text Mom yet.

- Cooperate with the police officer. Show him your passport and explain that you have not made the best decisions in the past, and you need to make a fresh start. Tell him you have decided that California is the place to do it.

- The officer will say, "I'm not supposed to do this, but hop in; I will give you a ride to the end of my territory."

Text Mom: Found a ride. I'm okay.

STEP 6:

When the nice officer leaves you off at the convenience store at the end of his territory, make friends with the store clerk.

- By now, it's midnight. You are already sore from carrying so much.

- Take 15 minutes at the store to rest and buy a water ($1.00).

- After leaving the store and walking only 200 yards, another kind officer will flash his blue lights, and ask, "Are you Kyle? Hop in; I can give you a ride to IH-10."

- Hop in and thank the police officer who has received a call from the previous police officer.

- This officer will drop you off at Denny's Restaurant that's open 24/7.

- Bid the officer a good morning as you disembark.

**Text Mom: Found another ride.
I'm still okay.**

STEP 7:

Make friends with the server working the back section of the restaurant.

- Tell server who you are, what you are doing, and why.
- He will say, "Take the booth in the back. What can I get you?"
- Tell him, "I have very little money. Maybe a glass of water."
- Accept his kind offer of coffee and water.
- Charge your cell phone and get a couple hours of sleep.

Text Mom: Found a place to spend the night.

- The server will wake you at 6:00 a.m. with pancakes on the house. He will bring you a piece of cardboard and a marker and say, "Every hitchhiker needs a sign."
- Write "West" on your sign.
- As you leave, he will hand you twenty dollars from his tips. And here's the tricky part: to accept it or not to accept it. Try to refuse the money.
- He will say, "Pay it forward, my friend."

**Text Mom:
Made a friend; insisted I take $20. Nice guy.**

STEP 8:

Walk 100 yards from Denny's to the corner of 46 and IH-10.

- Put your sign to use. Hold it at waist level.
- In 90 seconds or less, a rancher will stop and say, "Want a ride?"
- Gladly accept the ride.
- He will hand you a Whataburger sandwich and say, "This was an extra."
- To which you will say, "I can't pay for this."
- He will say, "Pay it forward, son."
- Ponder this phrase for future reference.
- Put sandwich in backpack for later.
- Enjoy the ride with the kind man who leaves you off at one of those Texas-friendly roadside rests.
- He will say, "Great place to get a ride with one of these truckers. Good luck to you, son, and happy journey."

Text Mom: In Kerrville. I'm still okay. Don't worry.

STEP 9:

Be mindful of how you carry your sign.

- Don't let it be too obvious; hold it at your side with the lettering facing out.

- Look for a trucker with a dog; as a rule, truckers who travel with a dog are pretty friendly people.

- You may have to sit at a picnic table and wait for two hours or more for a ride.

- Look at your phone. It is now 9:00 a.m. You may be a bit scared, but resist calling Mom for a ride home. Remember her words: "Don't call me from Kerrville at 9:00 a.m. and ask me to come get you."

- Watch as a trucker pulls in and a black and white dog jumps out of the cab.

- Ask the trucker if you can pet his dog. He will say, "Sure."

- Lay your sign down on the grass with the letters staring straight up.

- He will say, "I see you're going West. Where abouts?"

- You say, "I'm trying to start over in Oxnard, California."

- He will say, "Son, you're in luck. I'm going to LA. I'll take you the whole way."

BINGO! You're in!

Text Mom:

Found a trucker going all the way to Oxnard.

BUT YOU AREN'T THERE YET!

STEP 10:

Take turns riding shotgun with Oreo, the dog, since this is usually his favorite seat.

- When the dog is riding shotgun, you will sleep on the bed in back.

- Every time the trucker stops at a rest stop or at a gas station for gas, you will walk Oreo for him.

- In the afternoon, when the trucker stops for dinner, tell him you're not hungry. (You have $40 on you, but you're not sure when you will need it.) Besides, your stomach is a bit queasy from riding in the bed in back.

- When George, the truck driver, returns, he will have two hamburgers for you.

- He will say, "Here. Eat. You have to be hungry."

- You eat so he doesn't feel as though he has wasted his money.

**Text Mom: Had two burgers for dinner.
I'm okay.**

STEP 11:

Ride all night long in the bed with Oreo.

- The next stop will be Arizona. George will have to make a mandatory stop here for several hours.

- Now is the time to make some money. Since you have $40, take $10 and buy 5 scratch-off tickets. You will be lucky and make $20.

- Now you will have $50, since you spent $10 on the 5 tickets. This might be a lucky streak, so take $20 and buy 10 scratch-off tickets. You will make $40. Now you have $70.

Text Mom: Made $60 in scratch-off tickets. I'm okay; Don't worry.

- With this newfound fortune, insist on paying for George's breakfast. It's the least you can do.

- After breakfast and a refreshing walk with Oreo, and with a fistful of cash, settle into the truck for the last leg of the trip.

- Dream happy thoughts. Your luck just might be changing.

Text Mom: Bought George his breakfast. Next stop: L.A.

STEP 12:

George, Oreo and you pull into Los Angeles, California, at 4:00 Monday morning.

- Help George unhook the trailer full of office furniture.

- George will give you a lift to the bus station.

- Thank him for the ride and bid him goodbye.

- Don't forget to say goodbye to Oreo; he did share his bed with you.

- Be sure to get George's address: Mom will want to send him a thank you note.

- You have had good luck this far, so perhaps you can make it to Oxnard by yourself. Buy a bus ticket to Oxnard, California. It's $11. You can afford that.

  Text Mom: Leaving L.A. on a bus to Oxnard.

STEP 13:

You might make a wrong bus connection at this point and have to buy a different ticket. Now you have a problem.

- You paid $25 for that huge breakfast that you and George enjoyed in Arizona. You also bought some snacks and chewing tobacco—a habit that might be getting too expensive for you.

- Ask the lady at the ticket window, "How much to Oxnard?"

- She will say, "$15." Count your money. Thirty bucks.

- If you spend $15 for this ticket, you will have $15 left.

- Another lady will appear at the window; the two ladies will whisper to each other. They will probably be talking about you. Maybe you look tired. Maybe you smell bad.

- One of the ladies will say, "Hey, kid, we will buy your ticket for you. Just remember to pay it forward."

- Accept their generosity.

**Text Mom: Made more new friends.
I'm still okay.**

STEP 14:

Call your friend to let him know the bus will drop you off five minutes from his front door.

- When your friend decides he wants to hitchhike this summer from California to New York and invites you to go with him:

- Thank him for the invitation

- Kindly decline the offer

- Smile

- Consider that your easy 14-STEP hitchhiking trip had to have been a miracle

- Take an oath never to hitchhike again.

**Text Mom: In Oxnard.
I'm okay.
Love ya.**

The End

www.ingramcontent.com/pod-product-compliance
Lightning Source LLC
Chambersburg PA
CBHW071550080526
44588CB00011B/1858